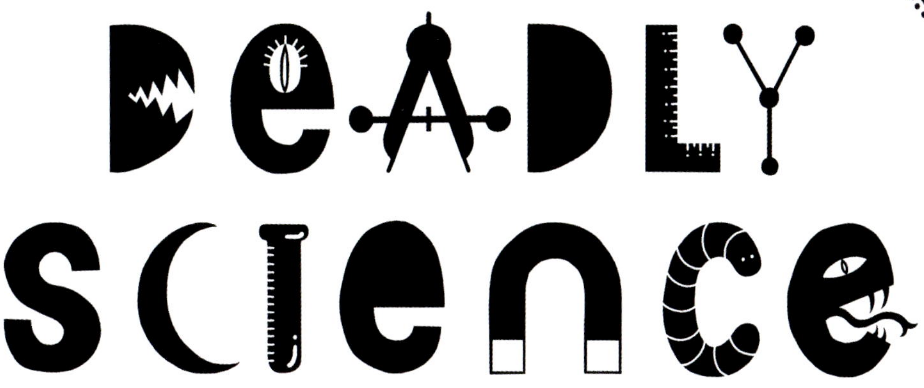

Animal adaptations

Contents

ADJUNCT ASSOCIATE PROFESSOR COREY TUTT OAM

DEADLYSCIENCE

DeadlyScience aims to provide Science, Technology, Engineering and Mathematics (STEM) resources to remote schools around Australia. So far, DeadlyScience has shipped more than shipped more than 33,000 STEM books and resources to more than 800 schools across the country.

The organisation began when proud Kamilaroi man Corey Tutt found out that some schools in Australia were completely under-resourced and that Aboriginal and Torres Strait Islander children were discouraged from pursuing STEM because of this. DeadlyScience knows from personal experience that books and resources change lives and believes these kids deserve nothing but the best. Aboriginal and Torres Strait Islander peoples in Australia were the First Scientists of this land, and DeadlyScience is committed to preserving that history.

Adaptations

An adaptation is any physical or behavioural characteristic of a living thing that helps it to survive. These features are designed to suit the environment in which a plant or animal lives. Adaptations may help an organism to survive in hot or cold weather, negotiate difficult terrain, find food or stay hidden from predators.

DID YOU KNOW?

In Pitjantjatjara, an Anangu language from Central Australia, this lizard is known as ngiyari (nee-ah-ree).

THORNY DEVIL

Anatomical adaptations

An anatomical adaptation involves some part of a living thing's body – the physical features of the organism. These include things you can see, such as the size of an animal, its covering (e.g. fur or feathers), colour and the way it moves. Anatomical adaptations can also be hidden inside an animal, such as a layer of blubber to keep the animal warm in cool environments.

The thorny devil is covered in a network of scale grooves that allow it to stand in a puddle and pull water up along its legs and body towards its mouth, making the most of the little water available in arid areas.

Behavioural adaptations

The ways in which an animal behaves in order to survive in its natural habitat are known as its behavioural adaptations. These can be instinctive, something the animal knows to do from birth, or learnt from older animals, such as communication, hunting, and using tools.

The thorny devil will locate an ant trail and sit right on top of it, eating thousands of ants in a single day.

Physiological adaptations

Physiological adaptations refer to the way an animal's body functions and how it reacts to its environment. This can include things such as producing venom or poison, or storing water for long periods in dry environments. The thorny devil generates a sticky saliva, which means it can lap up ants with ease.

DID YOU KNOW?
The name kookaburra comes from the Wiradjuri word guuguubarra.

Natural selection

Over time, species become increasingly well adapted to living in their particular habitat. Living things that are not well adapted to their environment have a lower chance of survival and are therefore less likely to breed and pass their traits on. Species more adapted to a habitat tend to live longer and reproduce at a higher rate, so their characteristics become more common. As this process occurs over many generations, significant changes in the species' appearance and behaviour take place over time.

For example, Australia's kingfisher species mostly have beaks that are strong, long and narrow, perfect for diving into the water to snatch up fish. Kingfishers with narrower beaks are likely to be better at catching fish, so they are therefore stronger and live longer than kingfishers with wider beaks.

The laughing kookaburra and the blue-winged kookaburra, however, don't dive into the water for food but pounce on insects, small rodents, reptiles and other creatures in the leaf litter. They have shorter, broader beaks that allow them to swallow most of their prey in a single gulp. They hold larger prey in their beaks, bashing it against rocks or tree trunks to break it up – so they need strong beaks.

Physical features

GECKO

Many animals are known for their weird and wonderful body parts or anatomical adaptations. From the smallest mite to the largest whale, each creature possesses features that help it survive in its environment.

GREEN TREE PYTHON

Scales

Have you noticed that scaly creatures tend to live in places where the temperature is warm? This is because scales developed as a method to cope with hot, dry climates. Made of keratin (the same material as fingernails), scales provide protection against predators, aid movement and allow many reptiles to retain moisture by preventing the evaporation of water through the skin.

Wings

Four animal groups – birds, bats, insects and extinct flying reptiles called pterosaurs – have (or had) the ability to fly. Flying animals can move through the air 10–20 times faster than that of a similar-sized animal on the ground. Wings provide an animal unique access to food and the ability to migrate easily.

WEDGE-TAILED EAGLE

Beaks

Beaks (or bills) exist in many shapes and sizes – each well suited to helping an animal find food and raise young in its particular environment. Some birds have short, cone-shaped beaks for picking up seeds. Birds of prey, such as the wedge-tailed eagle, have strong, sharp, curved beaks that are perfect for tearing into their prey's flesh.

Sticky feet

Many Australian animals possess unusual feet, but perhaps none more so than geckos, with their sticky feet. Many Australian gecko species are equipped with specialised pads under their toes. The pads, covered with microscopic brush-like structures, are designed to grip tiny irregularities in seemingly smooth surfaces. This means that geckos can scurry along walls, ceilings and windows.

Claws

Claws are common in the animal kingdom. Many species of lizards and birds make use of these sharp tools. Claws can be used for climbing (gripping onto surfaces like tree bark), fighting (striking the opposition) and for eating (grabbing and tearing food).

MAGPIE

Fur

Many animals are covered in fur that keeps them warm. Echidnas, for instance, have a layer of thick fur below their spines. Of course, humans have hair, but even mammals that don't look fluffy, such as seals, have a layer of sleek, oily fur that keeps them warm in the water.

Opposable thumb

Imagine life without your thumbs! Daily tasks such as turning a door handle, picking up a book or gripping a knife and fork would be extremely difficult. Humans possess opposable thumbs, which means that the thumb can move around to push against the fingers. This allows us to grasp and handle objects, proving very useful in getting around and eating food. Some animals also have opposable thumbs. Koalas have two on each hand, for climbing and grasping leaves.

FACT

Each koala has its own unique fingerprint. Koala prints can look so similar to human fingerprints that they can be mistaken for ours.

KOALA

DID YOU KNOW?

The word koala comes from the Dharug language words gula or gulamany, meaning 'no drink' – because the koala gets its water from the leaves it eats.

Defence tactics

Every animal needs a way to find food and avoid becoming a meal for some other species. Animals employ a number of tactics to survive in environments where competition for food is extreme.

Mimicry

Some animals act, sound or look like a different animal, usually to make them seem poisonous or dangerous. In many cases, mimicry is an attempt to deceive a predator, meaning it is an 'anti-predator' adaptation, but it can also be used to lure in prey. Mimicry can involve how an animal looks, behaves, sounds or smells. For example, the regent honeyeater has been recorded mimicking the noises of larger birds so it can be left to feed in peace.

REGENT HONEYEATER

Camouflage

The ability to blend into the environment is one of the most widespread methods of survival in the animal kingdom. Predators use the advantage of camouflage to sneak up on unsuspecting prey, while other animals do all they can to remain undetected by potential threats.

An animal that uses protective colouration usually has the same colour as its surroundings, making it difficult to single out. Protective resemblance is another form of camouflage in which an animal looks almost identical to its surroundings in colour but also in shape. Stick insects have an amazing body structure that makes them hard to tell apart from real twigs.

GOLIATH STICK INSECT

DID YOU KNOW?

Australia's goliath stick insect can reach up to 25 cm long – almost as tall as this page.

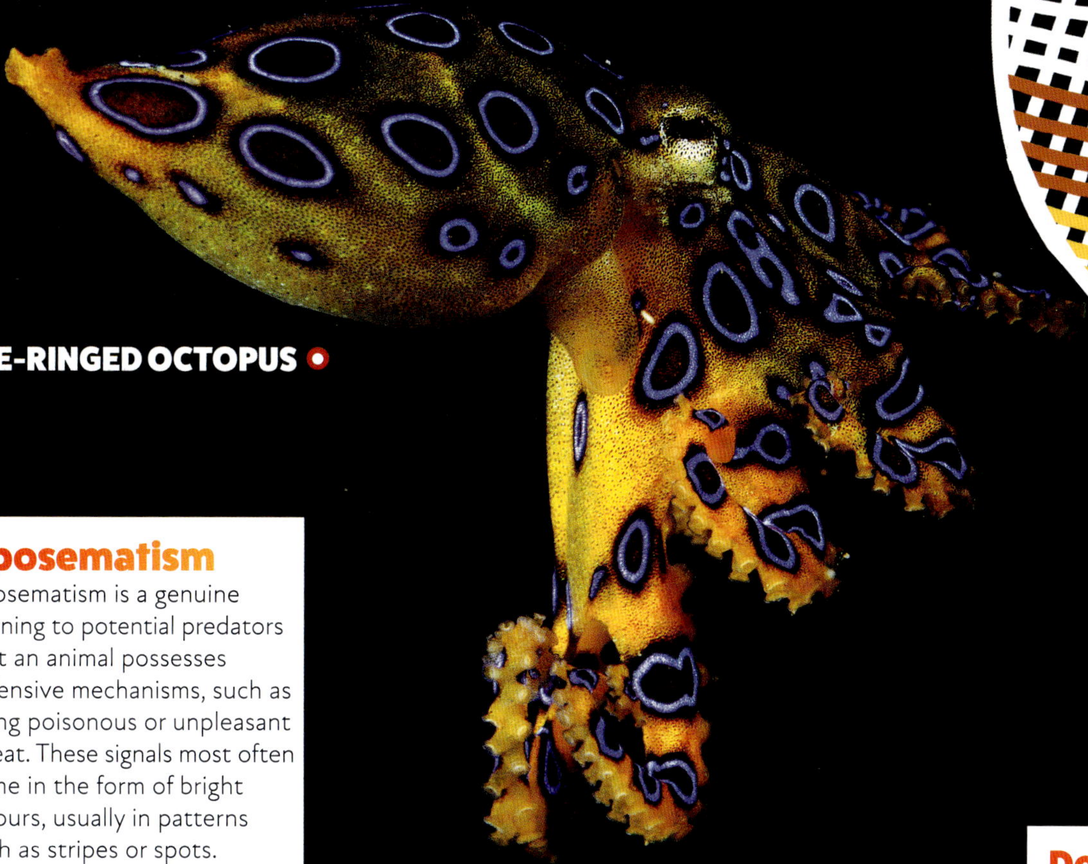

BLUE-RINGED OCTOPUS

Aposematism

Aposematism is a genuine warning to potential predators that an animal possesses defensive mechanisms, such as being poisonous or unpleasant to eat. These signals most often come in the form of bright colours, usually in patterns such as stripes or spots. The brighter the organism, the more toxic it may be.

If a predator does not heed the colourful warning, it may come up against a second form of defence – toxicity. The highly toxic blue-ringed octopus is an amazing example of this because its rings flash electric blue whenever it feels threatened.

Non-visual signs

Sounds and smells can be an effective way to put off predators or threats. Some animals produce warning noises from a distance, while others will become noisy once grabbed by a predator. Animals that use smell may stink out threats with strategic vomiting, or secretions such as spray or slime. The Tasmanian devil, for instance, can produce a pungent odour when threatened or stressed.

DID YOU KNOW?

In palawa kani, a language of Lutruwita, the Tassie devil is known as purinina.

TASMANIAN DEVIL

Deimatic behaviour

Another technique some animals use to intimidate predators and stop an attack is using a sudden display of colour or part of its body to distract or scare off a predator. In many cases, the display is a bluff, intended only to buy time for escape. For example, the frill-necked lizard is known for 'deimatic' displays in which its frill stretches open. It will open its mouth wide and raise itself up on its legs in order to seem larger and more threatening.

FRILL-NECKED LIZARD

Poison and venom

Venomous and poisonous don't mean the same thing. They refer to the way that the animal uses its toxic chemicals. Poisonous animals are passive, and the poisons are generally used by animals for defence. Venoms, on the other hand, are active and can be used to hunt prey and fight predators.

Poison

Poisonous organisms possess toxins that become dangerous to another organism when touched or eaten. These toxins can have a wide range of effects on their victims: from stunning them to damaging tissue material or even causing death. Poisons range in their levels of severity, and their impact will depend on the size of the victim.

Being poisonous is a defensive mechanism to prevent predation. Poison is present in a range of plant species, as well as in amphibians, sea creatures, and even some birds and mammals.

The beautiful mandarinfish, for example, is covered in tiny spines that inject a toxic mucus into anything that tries to handle or eat it. The mandarinfish doesn't have scales, so it would be extremely vulnerable if not for the thick layer of mucus covering it, which protects it from the elements and also from predators.

Another poisonous fish is the pufferfish. Famous for inflating its body with oxygen to deter would-be predators, it also generates a poison called tetrodotoxin. A single pufferfish contains enough tetrodotoxin to kill 30 humans.

Venom

Venom is a poison that is delivered by biting, stinging or injecting. Some types of venom can attack the brain and nervous system, while others attack the victim's cell structure, the cardiovascular system, or muscle tissue; they can also break down tissue. In general, venomous animals possess both special glands in which to make the venom, and something sharp to administer it with, such as spines, stingers or fangs. These animals include spiders, snakes, insects and sea creatures (jellyfish and coral). Australia is home to some of the world's most deadly venomous animals.

The inland taipan (also known as the fierce snake) has venom that contains nerve-damaging toxins that target muscle tissue, and another chemical that thins blood and leads to excessive bleeding. An average bite produces enough venom to kill 25–30 people, although there are no recorded fatalities because it is shy and tends to live in sparsely populated areas. Other animals, such as box jellyfish, have extremely toxic venom.

RAKALI

Fighting back

As is the case in the natural world, adaptation in one organism often prompts a reactionary development in another. Animals may develop a resistance to specific toxins so that they can keep eating certain plants or animals, or they develop a behavioural adaptation to work around it.

The rakali, a native water rodent, is one of the only Australian mammals that has learnt to eat toxic cane toads. The rats were found to target large toads, dissecting them to eat their hearts and livers while avoiding the poisonous skin and glands.

BOX JELLYFISH

PLATYPUS SPUR

DID YOU KNOW?

Male platypuses have a venomous spur above their hind feet, used mostly during fights with other males. Humans stung by a spur experience severe pain. The platypus has multiple Indigenous names, including boondaburra, mallingong and tambreet.

HUMPBACK WHALE

Seasonal changes

The conditions in a particular environment vary season to season. Some environments experience drastically different temperatures, levels of rainfall, daylight hours and a number of other shifting climate factors. Animals need to be able to adjust to changing seasonal conditions, whether by changing locations through migration or making other behavioural or physical adaptations.

DID YOU KNOW?

The Woppaburra people of the Keppel Islands know the humpback, their totem species, as mugga mugga.

Migration

Some animals are not equipped to cope with the changes that occur during seasonal cycles. These creatures move to a new location when their habitat becomes inhospitable. This behaviour is known as migration. Some animals follow the seasons to stay warm, and others follow the seasons to find food. Animals may also migrate to find a mate and reproduce.

Humpback whales migrate along the Australian coastline, spending the winter in tropical seas and the summer in Antarctic, krill-rich waters.

Hibernation/aestivation

Hibernation is an adaptation found in endothermic animals (those that can maintain an internal body temperature) often labelled as 'warm-blooded'. To conserve energy, often in cooler months, they lower their body temperature to just a fraction of their normal levels and remain in this state for extended periods. In Australia, four species of pygmy-possum, a handful of bat species, and the short-beaked echidna are all known to hibernate.

The eastern pygmy-possum – found along the coast from Queensland to South Australia and in Tasmania – has the longest hibernation of any mammal, spending a year in a less-active state.

Some animals enter a state similar to hibernation, but it is in warm, dry weather rather than winter. This is called aestivation or 'summer sleep', and it is seen in species such as the crucifix frog and the critically endangered western swamp tortoise.

DID YOU KNOW?

The crucifix frog also uses aposematism – its bright colours warn predators off.

Winter coats

Changes in season can bring about changes in the physical appearance of many animals. Just like us, when winter hits, animals tend to put on a warm coat – only for them, it is a natural change in their body. Feathers and fur that have provided a light coat in summer grow thicker, which provides insulation against cool temperatures. Alpine dingoes, for instance, have thicker winter coats than their more temperate-living cousins.

Working together

Social dynamics play a big role in the survival of animal species, so it is important that they form relationships to suit their particular environment, size and abilities. Some animals stick together in herds; others prefer a smaller family unit or going solo. Some animals even work with other species to survive.

CLOWNFISH

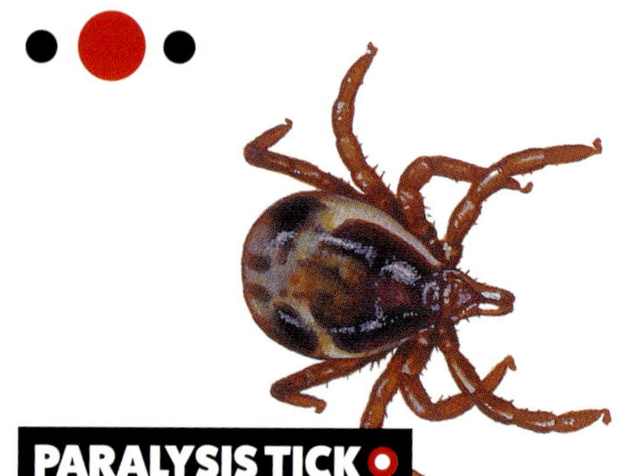

PARALYSIS TICK

SHINGLEBACK LIZARDS

POD OF ORCAS

Parasitism

Some relationships in the natural world are not so friendly. When one organism harms another without offering any benefit in return (but doesn't kill it), this is known as a parasitic relationship. In general, a parasite is much smaller than its 'host'. Examples include blood-sucking insects such as ticks and lice.

Mutualism

Relationships are not always confined to the same species. When two species benefit from a relationship, it is known as mutualism. One of the most well-known examples is the relationship between the anemone and the clownfish. Clownfish live inside anemones, which have stinging tentacles. The clownfish are covered in a mucus that prevents them from being hurt by the tentacles. The clownfish stay safe from predators while inside the anemones. The anemone benefits from the waste products of the fish, and also because the clownfish fend off any of the reef's hardier fishes that might try to eat the anemone.

The purple copper butterfly has a mutually beneficial relationship with a species of attendant ant. The butterfly lays her eggs near the ants, which protect the eggs. When the larvae hatch, the ants also guide them to food. In return, the ants feed on a sugary syrup that comes off the backs of the larvae.

Hunting parties

Many animal species are able to hunt more effectively by working together. Joining forces reduces the energy and risk involved for each individual. It also allows animals to take on much larger or more threatening prey than they would approach on their own. For example, dolphins sometimes work together by rounding up schools of fish or squid into a tight group, and then darting through the middle to feed. Pods of orcas have been known to swim in coordinated movements that create waves large enough to knock seals off floating ice.

Small families

Many animals live in small family groups. This has advantages over bigger groups, which can be easily spotted by predators, generate competition for food and mates, and can enable germs to spread.

Some animals live alone, preferring a primarily solitary existence. These animals are often very territorial and aim to avoid competition for the opportunity to mate or find a meal.

Shingleback lizards, sometimes referred to as the 'faithful lizard', are one of very few monogamous (having one mate) reptile species in the world. They live for up to 50 years, over which time they usually acquire a long-term partner that they stay close to for the rest of their lives.

DID YOU KNOW?

Budgerigars feature in the Tjukurrpa (Dreaming) depicted in the art of the Warlpiri people, whose country is centred in the Northern Territory's Tanami Desert. Here, budgies are known as ngatijirri and are a recurring motif in local artworks, offering clues to the location of water and ceremonial sites.

Large families

Some animals live together in big groups. Sticking together makes travelling safer and means they can share jobs such as finding food, watching out for danger and protecting their young.

Fish swim together in large groups called schools. This makes them look bigger, scaring off animals that might otherwise try to eat them.

Many animals in grassland environments live in herds, which also provides safety in numbers. If a predator approaches the herd, each individual's risk of being eaten is lowered by the sheer number of animals.

Many birds form flocks for safety. When it rains in the outback, budgerigars occasionally form flocks of millions of birds, flying in formations that deter larger birds of prey.

Insects such as ants and bees live in huge groups called colonies, in which each member has a specific job to carry out, such as defence.

Life in the dark

Some animals are more active at night than during the day, and some even prefer life underground in the dark. These animals have specialised adaptations that help them survive in dark places.

BARKING OWL

Nocturnality

Have you ever wondered where the term 'night-owl' comes from? Used to describe people who stay awake late into the night, the term reflects the pattern of activity commonly exhibited by owls, in which they are active during the night but then sleep during the day.

Such animals are nocturnal, a clever way to avoid heat and daytime predators and to find certain prey.

To cope in the dark, nocturnal creatures have evolved impressive senses of hearing, smell and sight. Nocturnal animals include species of possum, quoll, owl and bat.

Animals that follow the opposite pattern of activity and behaviour (such as humans, who are awake by day and sleep at night) are known as diurnal.

DID YOU KNOW?

First Nations peoples from Western Australia have several names for this owl, including goordemul, woolboogle and woorup.

LETTER-WINGED KITE

RUFOUS BETTONG

DID YOU KNOW?

The world's only truly nocturnal hawk, the letter-winged kite, hunts by moonlight. Courting, nesting and egg hatching are all synchronised to the Moon's cycles.

Going underground

In some circumstances, choosing to be active during the night rather than in daylight is not enough to ensure survival. Some creatures live underground, where they can avoid extreme temperatures, hide from predators and find worms, roots and insect eggs to eat.

Some animals spend time both above and below ground, such as bilbies. Others, such as cicadas during their nymph stage, spend a certain phase of their life underground. Yet others spend almost their entire lives underground, such as the itjaritjari.

Also known as the southern marsupial mole, it is ingeniously adapted to desert life. Unlike most burrowing mammals, itjaritjaris don't make permanent burrows. Instead, they dig and backfill as they go, carving a hole in the sand ahead with spade-like fore feet and pushing the loosened sand back behind themselves with slightly webbed hind feet. At the same time, they squeeze their tubular body forward a few centimetres at a time. They are completely blind and use their calloused nose and forehead as a ram.

Eyeshine

Many nocturnal animals and deep-sea animals have a specialised layer of tissue at the back of their eyeballs that reflects light back through the retina. This allows animals such as owls and sharks to see clearly in dim light. This iridescent layer is what creates eyeshine – the glow that is visible in some animals' eyes when they catch the light or are photographed in a certain way.

ITJARITJARI

DID YOU KNOW?

The itjaritjari is an important ancestral creature for the Aṉangu people of the Red Centre, featuring in the Dreaming of several other First Nations groups as well.

Extreme weather

Extreme weather events such as cyclones, floods, fires and tsunamis are an increasingly regular part of life that animals have had to adapt to. Such damaging occurrences are influenced by the weather patterns El Niño and La Niña. El Niño results in drier months and often in droughts and bushfires. La Niña is essentially the reverse weather pattern, featuring storms and floods.

BLACK KITE

FLAME ROBIN

Fires

Fires are a fact of life in Australia, and many of our animals have strategies to cope with bushfires or even benefit from them.

When bushfires strike, large mammals such as kangaroos usually head for safety near water. Sometimes, they even double back across the fire front to shelter in an already burnt area. Other smaller animals might sneak into a wombat burrow or hollow tree, sheltering underground from the heat.

Shinglebacks and fat-tailed dunnarts are among the species that have been found to wake up or respond to the smell of smoke, while some Australian frog and bat species have woken up (even from a state of torpor) at the mere sound of fire.

After the fires, some animals, such as the yellow-tailed black-cockatoo and flame robin, return to a fire-affected area to feed on insects and regenerating plants. Fire-beetles flock to burnt areas from as far as 130 km away to lay their eggs in the wood of burnt trees.

If they have the ability, some mammals will enter a stage of torpor after a fire so they won't need as much food while it is scarce.

DID YOU KNOW?

In a Gunai Kurnai Dreaming story, the flame robin got his bright chest when he returned fire to the people from a thieving spirit.

Firehawks

Australia's remarkable 'firehawks', which include black kites, whistling kites and brown falcons, take coping with fire a step further. These birds pick up smouldering sticks from fires and drop them in unburnt areas to spread the fire further. This flushes out insects and small mammals that they can then swoop down on and eat.

Droughts

Australia is frequently in drought – periods of serious shortage of water. At their worst, droughts in Australia have spanned thousands of square kilometres and lasted for years. Because all animals need water, drought often leads to widespread wildlife fatalities. However, some animals have clever adaptations to help them survive periods of drought.

Although kangaroos are prolific breeders in good times, they have evolved a clever way to cope with the tough times: they can hit 'pause' on pregnancy, halting the growth of a joey midway through development if conditions aren't good and then nursing multiple joeys when times are better.

WATER-HOLDING FROG

Water-holding frog

This frog inhabits the continent's driest areas, hunting in gilgais (cracked clay depressions) after rain for insects, shrimps and tadpoles. It waits out dry times underground, living for up to seven years on the fat and water trapped in its tissues and under its skin. While there, it secretes a wax-like substance that forms a cocoon around the frog, preventing any moisture loss.

The water-holding frog has long been used by First Nations people as a water source. Able to locate the frog underground, they have been known to squeeze the water out of the frog's bladder to drink when in need of hydration. This frog is thought to be linked to the Dreaming story of Tiddalik the thirsty frog, found in many parts of Australia.

DID YOU KNOW?

The Tiddalik Dreaming story, told in many parts of Australia, is about a greedy frog who drinks up all the water.

Cane toad case study:

Purnululu School

Western Australia's Purnululu Aboriginal Independent Community School joined the University of Queensland's research project 'Cane Toad Challenge'. This partnership involved the school being supplied with detailed instructions on how to build a cane toad trap and a supply of baits to attract cane toads. The school's contribution to the research was to provide data on their collecting.

Cane toads are not native Australian animals. They are originally from rainforests in South and Central America. In 1935, 102 cane toads were introduced to Australia in north Queensland. They were brought here to eat the cane beetle, which was affecting sugarcane crops.

Because of their particular adaptations, as well as the welcoming Australian environment, there are now hundreds of millions of cane toads in Australia. Cane toads are poisonous, so native animals that eat them (which would help keep the numbers down) can die after consuming them.

When cane toads were first introduced, they would increase their 'range' – the area in which they live – by about 10 km a year. Now, they spread at 40–60 km a year. Today's toads are bigger and have longer legs than those from 50 years ago. They have hopped 2500 km across the top of the country, all the way to Broome in Western Australia. They have spread to arid regions, and a colony is established as far south as Sydney.

Since they were introduced to Australia in 1935, cane toads have caused a lot of damage to our native animals. The high school students at Purnululu Aboriginal Independent Community School are trying to change that.

The students designed cane toad tadpole traps. The traps needed to be placed in shallow water. The tubs needed holes to be cut in the sides so funnels could be glued in. Each trap needed a lid, so it wouldn't get too hot in the trap. After making five traps, the students decided where the best places in the community's creeks would be. The traps were placed into the creeks, and baits were put into each trap. The baits were designed at the University of Queensland's Institute of Molecular Bioscience. Each bait lasted for 24 hours.

Cane toad tadpoles often eat cane toad eggs. The female covers the eggs with pheromones to keep them safe. The pheromones have a smell that attracts the cane toadlets. The researchers at the university used this to create baits. If baits are in tubs in shallow water, cane toad tadpoles think there are lots of eggs in the tubs. They swim into the tubs though the funnels and can't get out.

Every couple of days, the students took new baits to the creek, and the traps were checked.

JULIA MUNG AND POLLY NUNGATCHA

While the students didn't trap any tadpoles, they caught many cane toadlets. Each time they were at the creek, they looked for cane toads, tadpoles and eggs. Cane toad eggs are different to native frog eggs. The cane toad lays eggs in a long ribbon, with two rows of black eggs.

In the last term of 2020, the high school students caught almost 2000 cane toadlets. The cane toad is poisonous throughout its whole life, so the students always washed their hands after handling the toadlets. The toadlets were placed in a plastic tub and taken back to school. The students counted the toadlets they caught.

They researched cane toads and learnt that cane toads can adapt to live anywhere. They can eat anything, have no natural predators in Australia, and are deadly to animals that eat them. The students learnt that cane toads can lay up to 30,000 eggs twice a year.

– Carol Laverty, Purnululu Aboriginal Independent Community School, Western Australia.

CANE TOADLETS

FROG HOLLOW SPRING, WA

DID YOU KNOW?

Some native species, such as planigales, barramundi and marbled frogs, have learnt to avoid eating cane toads.

DID YOU KNOW?

In the Djiru language, the name for this flightless bird is gunduy; jina gunduy means 'cassowary footprint'.

In the rainforest

Rainforests are dense forests usually found in wet, warm climates not far from the equator. They feature tall trees, a huge variety of plants and animals, and plenty of rain. They are perfect habitats for animals and plants, and they are home to more varieties of species than anywhere else on Earth.

Southern cassowary

Standing a towering 1.8 m tall, the southern cassowary stalks the northern Queensland rainforest and is responsible for transporting the seeds of more than 60 plant species around Cape York Peninsula.

These large birds have tough skin and bristly feathers, which protect them from spiny vegetation and allow them to crash through dense rainforest to disappear quickly from view.

They also have a sharp, elongated claw on each foot, which is used in territorial disputes or as a method of defence.

FACT

Unlike other macropods, which have one at a time, female musky rat-kangaroos often birth 1–3 joeys per litter, even twins or triplets!

Musky rat-kangaroo

The world's smallest kangaroo lives in the rainforests of north-eastern Australia. It bounds like a rabbit, rather than hopping like a kangaroo. It has an opposable first toe, a feature that other marsupials share but that other kangaroos do not. It uses this toe, as well as its prehensile tail, for climbing.

It is an important gardener, hiding fruits and seeds in scattered locations, which this marsupial often later forgets. This protects the seeds from being eaten by anything, improving the chances of seed germination for rainforest plants.

Grey-headed flying-fox

Most commonly spotted when flying along the horizon at sunset, the grey-headed flying-fox is a keystone species, and a critical part of the ecosystem on the east coast because of the role it plays in seed dispersal and pollination.

It hangs from tree branches, using the strong, curved claws on its feet and the tendons in its legs to easily lock itself into place. Its wings are evolved hands with a thin membrane stretched over the bones. When a flying-fox lets go of a branch, it basically drops straight into flight.

Red-eyed green tree frog

This frog lives in the rainforest canopy, coming down to breed after rain. Its long legs and large toe pads help it to climb up into the canopy.

It's been known to launch itself from a high branch after insects and land safely many metres below. Extensive webbing on its feet and its adoption of a glider-like posture in midair suggest the species may be developing the ability to control such descents.

Boyd's forest dragon

This beautiful lizard has a remarkable adaptation. Unlike most lizards, which control their temperature by basking in the sunshine, this rainforest resident (known as jalbil to the Kuku Yalanji people of the Daintree Rainforest region) lets its temperature shift with the ambient temperature around it.

One important impact of this adaptation is that its main predator, the amethystine python, can't use its specialised heat-seeking senses to spot a Boyd's forest dragon in the vegetation.

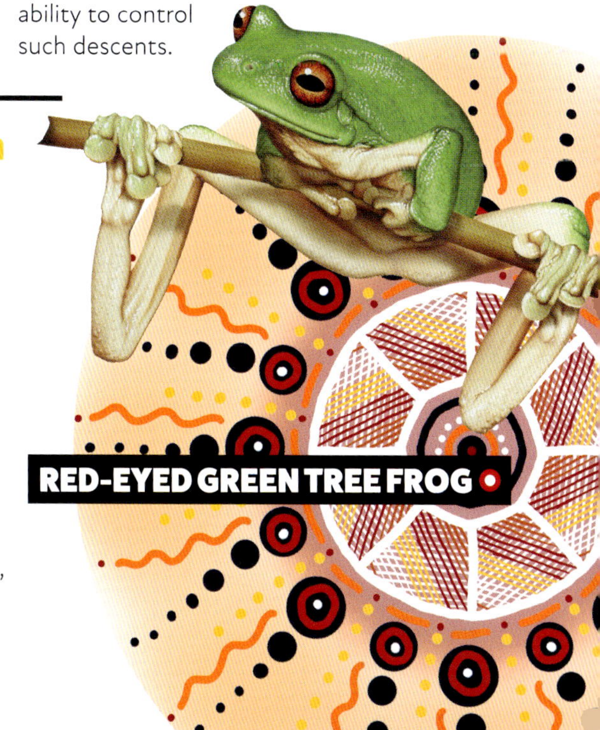

In the oceans

Covering more than 70% of the Earth's surface, the ocean is home to an extremely diverse range of inhabitants. Life began in the ocean, and plants and animals survive there in the deepest and darkest trenches, all the way to the surface. A myriad of predators and a range of environments, from vibrant coral reefs to polar regions, mean that ocean-dwelling organisms have developed unique survival methods.

HAWKSBILL TURTLE

Hawksbill turtle

Many deep-sea animals are bioluminescent, producing their own light to attract mates, camouflage themselves, defend against predators, or to lure prey closer. However, one of Australia's sea turtles, the hawksbill, was the first reptile found to display biofluorescence, reflecting the blue light that hits it as red and green. Because the hawksbill resides in coral reefs that also biofluoresce, this helps keep these turtles camouflaged.

Australian sea lion

These pinnipeds are 'benthic feeders' – they feed on the ocean floor. Young sea lions stay with their parents for up to 18 months, learning how to find and catch food. They have a thin layer of blubber under their skin that keeps them warm and also makes them more buoyant in the water.

AUSTRALIAN SEA LION

LEAFY SEADRAGON

Leafy seadragon

Delicate leafy seadragons are fish that live nowhere else in the world except the shallow coastal waters of southern Australia. Their main habitats are rocky reefs covered with kelp and other seaweed. Being coloured yellow and brown like the plants they swim among helps hide seadragons from predators. But their camouflage goes so much further. They also have skin growths all over the body that look exactly like waving sea-plant leaves.

DID YOU KNOW?

The Yanyuwa people, from the Gulf of Carpentaria, know the hawksbill turtle as karrubu.

Sperm whales

Many creatures that live in the ocean actually need to breathe air above the surface in order to survive, including sea turtles and marine mammals. This poses a dilemma for animals that need to dive to great depths in search of food.

As an evolutionary solution, diving sea mammals, such as sperm whales, have developed the ability to store a lot more oxygen in their blood cells than other animals. Higher oxygen levels allow the sperm whale to remain submerged for about 90 minutes at a time.

Mimic octopus

Using colour-matching and shapeshifting, this clever cephalopod avoids the jaws of its predators. It imitates a range of creatures, including a poisonous flatfish scooting along the sea floor and a lionfish swimming with its toxic spines erect.

Perhaps its most incredible morph, however, is when imitating the venomous banded sea snake: it conceals six of its arms in the sand and raises the other two, now coloured with thick black and beige stripes, in opposite directions to resemble the reptile.

SPERM WHALE

MIMIC OCTOPUS

TRY IT YOURSELF

Learn more about how blubber works!

In the deserts

Classified by an annual rainfall of less than 25 cm, desert environments are one of the most extreme on Earth. Although many deserts are dry and hot – reaching temperatures of up to 50 °C – they can also become extremely cold at night. Despite harsh conditions, deserts are home to a vast array of animals that have developed amazing techniques to regulate their temperature and use less water.

BEAKED GECKO

Beaked gecko

Beaked geckos eat termites, which feed on spinifex, and very little else. Despite their soft skin and fragile appearance, these geckos are common arid-zone inhabitants, and their diversity across Australia's deserts is among the world's highest. These small-bodied, big-eyed lizards shun high temperatures and emerge only at night. They use old spider burrows as shelters and resurface every few weeks to gorge on termites.

DID YOU KNOW?

Sturt Stony Desert is home to the kowari, a small carnivorous marsupial, and the knife-footed frog, another of Australia's burrowing frogs.

FACT

Australia has more deserts than any other continent on the planet! Many of our native animal species are arid-adapted as a result.

STURT STONY DESERT

GREATER BILBY

SPINIFEX HOPPING MOUSE

Greater bilby

The greater bilby is among the largest of Australia's desert marsupials. Known as mankarr by the Martu people of central Western Australia, its enormous ears help with cooling as well as hearing.

It uses its strong front limbs and claws to dig twisting burrows at least 2 m deep – the corkscrew shape keeps them safe from goannas and other predators. The bilby emerges from below ground at night to forage for roots, seeds and insect larvae.

Grey falcon

This arid-zone resident is found only in Australia, and it appears to treat the continent's deserts as one massive home range that it patrols from high above, across vast distances. It uses thermals (a column of rising air) to rise 2–3 km into the air, and then it glides at a speed of 80 km/h to the next thermal. Its speedy flight also helps in catching prey – often birds, but also small mammals and reptiles.

Spinifex hopping mouse

This little rodent, also known as tarkawara in the Pitjantjatjara/Yankunytjatjara language, has a range of adaptations that help it survive desert conditions.

For one, it produces the most concentrated urine of any mammal in the world. Its pee is so concentrated that it's almost solid. The spinifex hopping mouse has highly specialised kidneys and can survive very long periods without the need to drink water. It gets all the moisture it needs from its diet.

GREY FALCON

Desert trilling frog

About 40 different species of frog have been recorded in arid Australia. One of the most widespread is the desert trilling frog, a species capable of surviving long drought periods by living underground in a state of aestivation. The frog stores water in glands beneath its skin and encloses itself in a protective cocoon made from sloughed-off skin cells. As soon as the land receives a little bit of rain, between 5–10 mm, it will come to the surface to rehydrate and find food before burrowing back down.

DESERT TRILLING FROG

DID YOU KNOW?

The grey falcon is known as boorga in the Noongar language of south-west Western Australia.

In the grasslands

Grasslands often occur between forests and deserts, where the rainfall is not high enough to produce a forest but not low enough to result in desert conditions. They are generally flat and open, with grass as the most common vegetation. With the exception of Antarctica, every continent on Earth has grasslands, which are also known as savannahs, steppes and prairies.

EMU

CONDAMINE EARLESS DRAGON

Emu

While their inability to fly might seem like a disadvantage, emus make up for it with their running abilities. Unlike ostriches, which have only two toes, the emu has three toes – and the extra one makes quite a difference. Having three toes allows an emu to make 180-degree turns at great speeds, which is very useful for outrunning predators.

Condamine earless dragon

Found on the remnant grasslands of the Darling Downs in Queensland, this small lizard is a patchy brown colour that helps it camouflage in grass. When it needs to survey its surroundings, it climbs to the top of a grass clump to look around.

The lizard uses burrows made by other small animals to shelter from high temperatures in summer and cool weather in winter. It uses a sit-and-wait approach to find prey, not wasting energy in chasing food, but snapping up any ants, beetles or crickets that come past.

WOMBAT

Wombat

Wombats are very territorial. They aim to make it as obvious as possible what territory is theirs. To do this, they find high places on which to defecate. These spots are roughly at nose height so that other wombats can identify where boundaries lie.

Nankeen kestrel

Also known as the Australian kestrel, the nankeen kestrel grows to about the size of a pigeon, making it one of the world's smallest kestrels. It's also one of just two types of raptor in the country to hunt using suspension, not speed.

The nankeen kestrel faces into the wind and uses its power to hover in place as it scouts for food. The key to the kestrel's hovering success is feathers that have evolved to be much stiffer than the feathers of other falcons, allowing them to better withstand bending in the wind.

Their wings also have specialised slots between the feathers, which let air through to reduce turbulence. It's so good at this 'wind-hovering' technique, it can keep its head perfectly still in midair.

DID YOU KNOW?

This monotreme (egg-laying marsupial) has many names, including bigibila (Gamilaraay), wandayali (Wiradjuri), yinarlingi (Warlpiri) and jana jana (Bundjalung).

Short-beaked echidna

These burrowing animals have developed claws to help them live underground. Their flat front claws can break logs and dig powerfully through the ground. The echidna's hind legs point backwards, which is useful for pushing dirt out of the way while burrowing, but it means they waddle awkwardly when they walk.

In alpine areas

On one of the driest, flattest continents on Earth, the Australian Alps stand out as special. Although our mountains are small by world standards, they create unique landscapes and ecosystems that are home to many native plants and animals not found anywhere else. Plants and animals need to be well adapted to cool summers and freezing winters.

SOUTHERN CORROBOREE FROG

Southern corroboree frog

The southern corroboree frog grows to just 2.5–3 cm. It derives its name from the black and bright-yellow stripes – corroboree is an adaptation of the Dharug word garaabara, which refers to a First Nations gathering involving dancing and singing, often with people decorated with body paint. On this frog, the bright colours are a sign to predators that it is dangerous to eat – it releases a toxic chemical from its skin.

Mountain pygmy-possum

During summer nights, this possum (weighing 35–80 g) clambers among boulders to feast on mountain plum pine, bogong moths and other insects to prepare for a long winter sleep. It's the only marsupial that hibernates for long periods under snow, avoiding the worst of the cold weather. During that hibernation, its body temperature drops to about 2 °C. These possums are only found in three small regions – Mt Bogong and Mt Buller in Victoria, and Mt Townsend in NSW.

Alpine spiny crayfish

Relatively little is known about this crayfish, which grows to 58 mm long, and is found only in the high country of Victoria, NSW and the ACT. It inhabits cool mountain streams, seeking refuge under rock ledges and in burrows at the water's edge. It isn't able to control its own body temperature, so its burrows can be up to 2 m into the ground.

Alpine water skink

Found only in a restricted range in the High Country of south-eastern Australia, this skink is critically endangered in Victoria. It lives in damp areas, particularly sphagnum bogs and wet heath, and it may enter the water when startled. Unlike many reptiles, it gives birth to live young rather than laying eggs.

MOUNTAIN PYGMY-POSSUM

ALPINE SPINY CRAYFISH

DID YOU KNOW?

The mountain pygmy-possum was thought to be extinct until new populations were discovered in the 1960s.

ALPINE WATER SKINK

In cities

Human development has caused some of the most significant changes to Earth's environments. Natural evolution of ecosystems can take thousands of years, while urbanisation can vastly alter a habitat in a tiny fraction of that time. As a result, wildlife populations have had to adapt to rapidly changing conditions and new challenges – with varying degrees of success.

Australian brush turkey

The natural range of the brush turkey stretches along the east coast of Australia from Far North Queensland to the Illawarra, south of Sydney. After several centuries of habitat loss and predation by cats and foxes, these birds are now determinedly reclaiming their historic range in urban Australian cities.

A male brush turkey will use its big feet to rake mulch, twigs, soil and sand into a carefully shaped compost heap. A typical brush turkey mound can measure up to 4 m in diameter and stand 1.5 m high. Each male will then mate with a number of females, and his mound might eventually contain up to 50 eggs. The male will tend to the eggs.

To achieve this, he first uses his beak as a probe, inserting it into the mound as far down as the level of the eggs. His palate acts as a thermometer, and depending on the temperature he senses, he will remove or add more leaf-litter as needed.

TRY IT YOURSELF

Track what birds visit your backyard or school playground!

Brushtail possum

The brushtail possum is a highly adaptable animal that is right at home in an environment we have unwittingly fashioned to suit both us and them.

It will happily feast by night on everything from rosebuds and magnolia flowers to unattended pet food, and by day, it considers unprotected roof cavities the perfect city condo.

Inner-city possums have a more varied diet than the usual rural possums' mainstay of eucalypt leaves, meaning that despite the threats from cars, cats and dogs, they probably enjoy a survival advantage.

BRUSHTAIL POSSUM

Australian magpie

Magpies are one of the most common birds you'll spot in Australian cities. They're very intelligent, and their amusing antics are known to include play-fighting, sunbathing, frolicking in sprinklers and swinging from washing lines.

Although they are pretty tame for most of the year, their spring breeding season is accompanied by fiercely protective behaviour. Some magpie dads defend their nestlings by swooping down in a feathered black-and-white fury, bringing terror to unsuspecting walkers and cyclists.

Eastern water dragon

Water dragons live along almost every watercourse in eastern Australia. They're not fussy – pristine rivers, polluted suburban creeks, even ornamental ponds will support populations.

Away from urban areas, they're shy and difficult to approach, but city-slicker dragons are different. They have grown used to us and readily accept handouts.

In Brisbane's City Botanic Gardens, these dragons have flourished, with the population now numbering several hundred. The water dragons there are growing substantially bigger than non-urban water dragons.

EASTERN WATER DRAGON

AUSTRALIAN MAGPIE

DID YOU KNOW?

The magpie is known as coolbardie in the Noongar language.

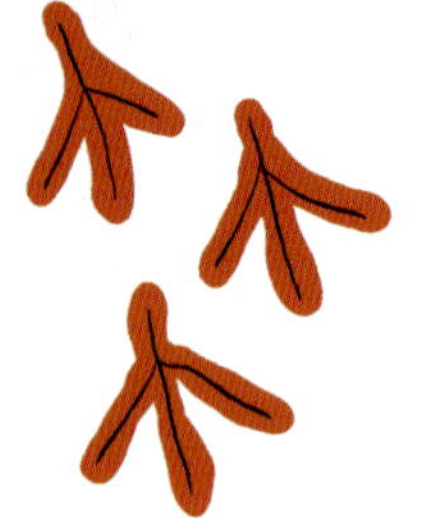

DEADLY SCIENCE

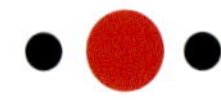

Animal adaptations

First published in 2021, reprinted in 2022, 2023

52–54 Turner Street
Redfern NSW 2016

editorial@ausgeo.com.au
australiangeographic.com.au

Series Editor: Corey Tutt
Illustrations: Mim Cole / Mimmim

Commissioning Editor: Karin Cox
Chief Sub-Editor: Serene Conneeley
Proofreader: Michele Perry
Creative Director: Aleksandra Beare
Designer: Hannah Chapman
Print Production: Andy Franks

AUSTRALIAN GEOGRAPHIC
Managing Director: David Haslingden
Director of Content: Liz Ginis
Licensing and Publishing Manager: Tom Bates
Commercial Assistant: Felicity McManus

Printed in China by LEO Paper Products LTD.

A catalogue record for this book is available from the National Library of Australia

Picture credits

Front Cover: Dan Sheridan/Australian Geographic (AG); Michelle D. Milliman/Shutterstock (SS); Ego Guiotto/AG; alslutsky/SS; Michael Payne/AG; ChameleonsEye/SS; Valt Ahyppo/SS; **2:** Kristian Bell/SS; **3:** Ken Griffiths/SS; Kevin Stead/AG; **4:** Paul Looyen/SS; Dr Steven Murray/SS; Dean Bracht/SS; Ego Guiotto/AG; Ego Guiotto/AG; fotandy/SS; **5:** Drew Hopper/AG; R Bain/SS; **6:** Andreas Ruhz/SS; Ken Browning/SS; **7:** SChantra/SS; Matt Cornish/SS; Bernhard Richter/SS; **8:** GoodFocused/SS; fenkieandreas/SS; Anastasia Mangindaan/SS; **9:** Nick Rains/AG; D. Cunningham/SS; Slomotiongli/CanvaPro (CP); **10:** Napong Suttivilai/SS; **11:** Bill Bachman/AG; Andrew Gregory/AG; Pawel Papis/SS; **12:** Mike McCoy/AG; Willyam Bradberry/SS; reptiles4all/SS; Ego Guiotto/AG; **13:** Leonarda Gonzalez/SS; Catzatsea/SS; **14:** Terry Dell/SS; **15:** Agami Photo Agency/SS; Mitch Reardon/AG; Auscape/Getty; **16:** Martin Helgemeir/Dreamstime; Rich Lindie/SS; **17:** Chris Ison/SS; Ken Griffiths/SS; **18:** Jason Edwards/AG; **19:** Carol Laverty/Purnululu Aboriginal Independent Community School (PAICS); Carol Laverty/PAICS; Esther Beaton/AG; **20:** Bancha Sae-Lao/SS; **21:** Ken Griffiths/SS; Grahame McConnell/AG; Kevin Stead/AG; Kevin Stead/AG **22:** Thierry Eidenweil/SS; John Ceulemans/SS; David Gruber; **23:** wildestanimal/SS; orlandin/SS; **24:** WiseLum/CP; Janelle Lugge/SS; **25:** Ken Griffiths/SS; Jiri Lochman/AG; LiquidGhoul/SS; Nicolas Day/AG; **26:** Lukas Vejrik/SS; retofuerst/SS; Steve Wilson/AG; Jiri Lochman/AG; **27:** Wayne Butterworth/SS; **28:** Leelakajonkij/SS; Kevin Stead/AG; **29:** Ego Guiotto/AG; Mark Jekabsons/NatureMapr/CC-BY-3.0; © Tim/iNaturalist; **30:** Esther Beaton/AG; **31:** Esther Beaton/AG; doublelee/SS; Rob D The Baker/SS.

Support trusted, independent, Australian-owned media with a focus on celebrating Australia through compelling stories of its people, places, and natural environment.

Australian Geographic contributes 100% of its profits to the Australian Geographic Society, including its conservation and sustainability programs.

We seek to inspire Australians to love and care for our country and, through the support of the Australian Geographic Society, to empower individuals and organisations to tackle environmental challenges and find innovative solutions to the many threats faced by our natural world.

AUSTRALIAN GEOGRAPHIC SOCIETY
Enquiries about sponsorship and donations:
02 9136 7206
Email: society@ausgeo.com.au
www.australiangeographic.com.au/society

AUSTRALIAN GEOGRAPHIC SUBSCRIPTIONS
Sales and customer enquiries: 1300 555 176
australiangeographic.com.au/product-category/subscriptions